NEO-MEDROL

GW00454938

A Comprehensive Guide To Its Composition, Efficacy, And Insights Into Skincare Solutions

Gabriel Rivera

Contents

CHAPTER 1

INTRODUCTION TO ACNE AND SKIN CONDITIONS

Acne is a common skin condition that affects millions of people worldwide, regardless of age or gender.

It is characterized by the appearance of pimples, blackheads, whiteheads, and, in more severe cases, cysts and nodules. Beyond its physical impact, acne can also take a toll on an individual's emotional well-being and self-esteem.

UNDERSTANDING ACNE

Acne occurs when hair follicles become clogged with dead skin cells, excess oil (sebum), and bacteria. The exact causes of acne are multifactorial and can include hormonal imbalances, genetics, diet, stress, and environmental factors. While it often starts during adolescence due to hormonal changes, acne can persist into adulthood and, in some cases, even emerge later in life.

TYPES OF ACNE

Acne can manifest in various forms, each with its unique characteristics. Common types of acne include:

a. Comedones:

Non-inflammatory acne lesions, divided into open comedones (blackheads) and closed comedones (whiteheads).

b. Papules and Pustules:

Inflammatory acne lesions that appear as red, swollen bumps or pus-filled bumps on the skin. c. Nodules and Cysts:

Severe, deep-rooted inflammatory lesions that can cause pain and scarring.

IMPACT OF ACNE

Acne's impact extends beyond physical blemishes. It can lead to psychological effects such as reduced self-confidence, social anxiety, and even depression. Adolescents, in particular, may experience difficulties in forming relationships and coping with the changes occurring during this critical stage of development.

CURRENT ACNE TREATMENTS

Over the years, various treatments have been developed to manage acne, ranging from topical creams and gels to oral medications, antibiotics, and hormonal therapies. Each treatment approach targets different aspects of acne's pathogenesis, aiming to unclog pores, reduce inflammation, and control sebum production.

THE ROLE OF NEO MEDROL

Among the myriad acne treatments available, Neo Medrol stands out as a widely used option known for its effectiveness in managing acne symptoms. Neo Medrol is a topical medication that combines an antibiotic (neomycin) and a corticosteroid (methylprednisolone), working synergistically to address both bacterial infection and inflammation associated with acne.

UNDERSTANDING NEO MEDROL

we will delve into the specifics of Neo Medrol, exploring its composition, mode of action, and how it differentiates itself from other acne treatments.

NEO MEDROL COMPOSITION

Neo Medrol is a topical medication that combines two active ingredients: neomycin and methylprednisolone. Let's take a closer look at each component:

Neomycin: Neomycin is an antibiotic that belongs to the aminoglycoside class. It works by inhibiting the growth and spread of bacteria, including the types commonly associated with acne, such as Propionibacterium acnes. By reducing bacterial colonization on the skin, neomycin helps prevent the formation of new acne lesions and contributes to the overall improvement of the condition.

Methylprednisolone: Methylprednisolone is a corticosteroid, which is a type of anti-inflammatory medication. When applied topically, it helps reduce inflammation in the affected areas of the skin. Inflammatory responses play a crucial role in the development of acne lesions, so by targeting inflammation, methylprednisolone helps alleviate redness, swelling, and discomfort associated with acne.

MODE OF ACTION

The combination of neomycin and methylprednisolone in Neo Medrol offers a multifaceted approach to acne management. The mode of action can be summarized as follows:

Antibacterial Effect: Neomycin's antibacterial properties target the bacteria involved in acne formation. By inhibiting bacterial growth and activity, Neo Medrol helps to control the infection and prevent the worsening of existing lesions.

Anti-Inflammatory Effect: Methylprednisolone's anti-inflammatory action complements the antibacterial effect by reducing the inflammation caused by acne.

This helps soothe the skin, lessen redness, and promote faster healing of existing lesions.

CHAPTER 2

NEO MEDROL VS. OTHER ACNE TREATMENTS

Neo Medrol sets itself apart from other acne treatments through its combination of an antibiotic and a corticosteroid in a single topical formulation. This unique blend of active ingredients allows Neo Medrol to address both the bacterial component and the inflammatory aspect of acne simultaneously. By tackling these two critical factors, Neo Medrol offers a comprehensive approach to managing acne, which may lead to more rapid and noticeable results.

However, it's essential to note that Neo Medrol may not be suitable for all individuals or all types of acne. Different skin types and conditions may respond differently to various treatments, and in some cases, other topical or systemic medications may be more appropriate.

CLINICAL STUDIES AND EFFICACY OF NEO MEDROL

In this chapter, we will explore the scientific studies and evidence supporting Neo Medrol's effectiveness in treating acne. Understanding the research behind Neo Medrol will provide valuable insights into its efficacy and potential benefits.

EFFICACY STUDIES

Numerous clinical studies have been conducted to assess the efficacy of Neo Medrol in managing acne. These studies typically involve groups of participants with varying degrees of acne severity who are treated with Neo Medrol for a specific duration. The results are then compared to baseline measurements to evaluate the product's effectiveness.

REDUCTION IN ACNE LESIONS

One of the primary outcome measures in efficacy studies is the reduction in acne lesions. These lesions include comedones (blackheads and whiteheads), papules, pustules, nodules, and cysts. Neo Medrol's combination of neomycin and methylprednisolone targets both bacterial infection and inflammation, which can contribute to a significant reduction in the number and severity of acne lesions.

IMPROVEMENT IN INFLAMMATORY SYMPTOMS

Inflammatory acne lesions can cause redness, swelling, and tenderness. Neo Medrol's anti-inflammatory properties help alleviate these symptoms, leading to improved overall skin appearance and increased comfort for individuals undergoing treatment.

POSITIVE USER FEEDBACK

In addition to clinical studies, user feedback and testimonials play a crucial role in understanding the real-world effectiveness of Neo Medrol. Positive experiences from individuals who have used Neo Medrol can offer valuable insights into its efficacy and help potential users make informed decisions about its suitability for their needs.

Considerations and Limitations

While Neo Medrol has shown promising results in many cases, it's essential to consider that individual responses to treatments can vary. Some individuals may experience significant improvements, while others may not respond as favorably. Additionally, like any medication, Neo Medrol may have potential side effects, and not all individuals may be suitable candidates for its use.

PROFESSIONAL GUIDANCE

Before starting any acne treatment, including Neo Medrol, it is crucial to consult a healthcare professional or a dermatologist. They can evaluate your skin condition, consider your medical history, and recommend the most appropriate treatment plan for your specific needs.

Overall, the clinical studies and user feedback on Neo Medrol suggest that it can be an effective option for managing acne, particularly for individuals with mild to moderate forms of the condition. However, individual responses may vary, and professional guidance is essential to ensure safe and optimal treatment outcomes.

SAFETY AND SIDE EFFECTS OF NEO MEDROL

In this chapter, we will explore the safety profile of Neo Medrol, discussing potential side effects and precautions to consider when using this medication. Understanding the safety aspects of Neo Medrol is crucial for responsible and informed usage.

COMMON SIDE EFFECTS

Neo Medrol is generally considered safe when used as directed, but like any medication, it may cause side effects in some individuals. Common side effects that may occur with Neo Medrol include:

- Mild skin irritation, such as redness, itching, or dryness at the application site.

- Burning or stinging sensation upon application.

These side effects are usually mild and temporary, resolving as the skin gets accustomed to the medication. If you experience persistent or severe irritation, it's essential to discontinue use and consult your healthcare professional.

CHAPTER 3

ALLERGIC REACTIONS

While uncommon, some individuals may be allergic to certain components of Neo Medrol. Allergic reactions can manifest as itching, rash, swelling, or difficulty breathing. If you experience any signs of an allergic reaction after applying Neo Medrol, seek immediate medical attention.

PRECAUTIONS AND WARNINGS

To ensure the safe use of Neo Medrol, consider the following precautions:

- Avoid using Neo Medrol on broken or irritated skin.

- Do not apply Neo Medrol near the eyes, mouth, or mucous membranes.

- Neo Medrol may make the skin more sensitive to sunlight. Use sunscreen and protective clothing while using the medication to reduce the risk of sunburn.

INTERACTIONS WITH OTHER MEDICATIONS

Inform your healthcare professional about any other topical or oral medications you are using, as there is a potential for drug interactions. Certain medications or substances may interact with Neo Medrol, affecting its effectiveness or increasing the risk of side effects.

PREGNANCY AND BREASTFEEDING

If you are pregnant, planning to become pregnant, or breastfeeding, discuss the use of Neo Medrol with your healthcare professional. They can assess the potential risks and benefits and provide guidance on safe usage during these periods.

DISCONTINUING USE

If you experience any severe side effects or allergic reactions, discontinue use immediately and seek medical attention. Additionally, if your acne does not improve or worsens after using Neo Medrol as directed, consult your healthcare professional for further evaluation and alternative treatment options.

INDIVIDUAL CONSIDERATIONS

Remember that individual responses to Neo Medrol can vary. Some individuals may experience significant improvement in their acne symptoms, while others may find better results with different treatments. It's essential to work closely with your healthcare professional to determine the most suitable acne management plan for your specific needs.

By being aware of potential side effects and following the recommended precautions, you can use Neo Medrol responsibly and maximize its benefits in managing acne.

Practical Usage and Application of Neo Medrol

Understanding the proper dosage, application methods, and recommended treatment duration will help you make the most of Neo Medrol's potential in achieving clearer and healthier skin.

RECOMMENDED DOSAGE

The recommended dosage of Neo Medrol may vary depending on the severity of your acne and your healthcare professional's assessment. It is crucial to follow your doctor's instructions and the guidelines provided on the medication's packaging.

APPLICATION METHOD

Before applying Neo Medrol, thoroughly cleanse the affected area with a mild cleanser and pat dry. Be sure to avoid using harsh or abrasive cleansers that could irritate the skin further.

Using clean hands, apply a thin layer of Neo Medrol to the affected areas. It is best to focus on individual pimples or acne-prone regions rather than applying the medication to the entire face, especially if only specific areas require treatment.

Avoid applying Neo Medrol near the eyes, mouth, or mucous membranes, as it may cause irritation.

FREQUENCY OF APPLICATION

The frequency of Neo Medrol application may vary based on your doctor's recommendation and the product's instructions. In some cases,

Neo Medrol may be applied once or twice daily. However, it's essential not to exceed the recommended frequency, as overuse may lead to increased skin irritation.

DURATION OF TREATMENT

The duration of Neo Medrol treatment can also vary depending on the individual's response to the medication. In most cases, acne treatments require consistent use over several weeks to see noticeable improvements. However, if you notice any adverse effects or your acne worsens during treatment, contact your healthcare professional promptly.

COMBINING WITH OTHER ACNE TREATMENTS

Your healthcare professional may recommend using Neo Medrol in combination with other acne treatments, such as topical retinoids or benzoyl peroxide. Combining treatments can provide a more comprehensive approach to managing acne, targeting different aspects of the condition. However, it is essential to use these treatments as directed and to avoid combining products that may interact negatively.

CHAPTER 4

MONITORING PROGRESS

As you use Neo Medrol, monitor the progress of your acne regularly. Keep track of any changes in the number and severity of acne lesions, as well as the overall condition of your skin. If you have any concerns or questions about your progress, discuss them with your healthcare professional.

DISCONTINUING USE

If your acne improves and you achieve the desired results with Neo Medrol, your healthcare professional may recommend gradually reducing the frequency of application or discontinuing its use altogether. It's crucial to follow their guidance to ensure a smooth transition and prevent any potential acne flare-ups.

In conclusion, using Neo Medrol correctly and consistently, in accordance with your healthcare professional's recommendations, can contribute to achieving clearer and healthier skin. Remember that individual responses to treatment may vary, and some patience may be required as you progress on your acne management journey.

LONG-TERM MANAGEMENT AND MAINTENANCE OF CLEAR SKIN

In this chapter, we will discuss strategies for long-term management and maintenance of clear skin after successful treatment with Neo Medrol. Achieving clearer skin is a significant accomplishment, and adopting these practices can help you sustain those results and minimize the chances of acne recurrence.

MAINTAIN A CONSISTENT SKINCARE ROUTINE

Establishing a consistent and gentle skincare routine is essential for maintaining clear skin. This routine should include cleansing your face twice daily with a mild, non-comedogenic cleanser. Avoid harsh or abrasive products that can irritate the skin.

MOISTURIZE REGULARLY

Even if your skin tends to be oily, using a lightweight, oil-free moisturizer can help keep the skin hydrated without clogging pores. Proper hydration supports the skin's barrier function and can contribute to a healthier complexion.

SUN PROTECTION

Protect your skin from the sun's harmful UV rays by using a broad-spectrum sunscreen with an appropriate SPF rating. Sunscreen helps prevent sunburn and protects the skin from potential damage, which can exacerbate acne and lead to hyperpigmentation.

AVOID TOUCHING OR PICKING AT YOUR SKIN

Resist the urge to touch, squeeze, or pick at acne lesions, as this can worsen inflammation and may lead to scarring. Picking at the skin can also introduce bacteria and cause new breakouts.

BE MINDFUL OF YOUR DIET

While the relationship between diet and acne is not fully understood, some individuals find that certain foods may trigger or worsen breakouts. Be mindful of your diet and observe if certain food items seem to affect your skin. It can be helpful to maintain a balanced diet rich in fruits, vegetables, whole grains, and lean proteins.

Manage Stress

Stress can potentially exacerbate acne, as it may influence hormonal imbalances and trigger inflammatory responses. Engage in stress-reducing activities such as exercise, meditation, or hobbies that you enjoy.

REGULAR FOLLOW-UPS WITH YOUR HEALTHCARE PROFESSIONAL

Continuing to consult your healthcare professional or dermatologist for regular check-ups is crucial, even after your acne has improved. They can monitor your skin's progress, offer guidance on maintenance, and make adjustments to your skincare routine or treatment plan if needed.

CONSIDER REINTRODUCING SKINCARE PRODUCTS GRADUALLY

If you've been using a simplified skincare routine during active acne treatment, you can consider gradually reintroducing additional skincare products. When adding new products, introduce one at a time and observe how your skin responds. This helps identify if any particular product may be causing adverse reactions.

BE PATIENT AND KIND TO YOURSELF

Achieving clear skin is a journey that requires patience and self-compassion. It's normal to experience occasional breakouts, especially during hormonal fluctuations or periods of stress. Remember that maintaining clear skin is an ongoing process, and small setbacks do not diminish your progress.

By adopting these long-term management strategies, you can support the results achieved with Neo Medrol and enjoy clearer, healthier skin. Remember that every individual's skin is unique, and what works for one person may not work for another. Be open to adjusting your skincare routine as needed to find what best suits your skin's needs.

CHAPTER 5

USER TESTIMONIALS AND SUCCESS STORIES

In this chapter, we will share inspiring user testimonials and success stories of individuals who have benefited from using Neo Medrol in their acne management journey. These real-life experiences highlight how Neo Medrol has positively impacted their lives and provide encouragement for your own path to clearer skin.

Jessica's Story

Jessica, a 24-year-old professional, had struggled with persistent acne since her teenage years. She tried various over-the-counter products and prescription medications, but none seemed to provide the long-term relief she desired. Frustrated by her skin's condition, Jessica consulted a dermatologist, who recommended Neo Medrol as part of her acne management plan.

Within a few weeks of using Neo Medrol as directed, Jessica noticed significant improvements in her acne. The combination of neomycin and methylprednisolone seemed to work wonders for her, reducing both the number of acne lesions and the redness associated with inflammation. Jessica's self-confidence soared as she gained control over her acne, allowing her to focus more on her professional and personal life without feeling self-conscious.

Mark's Journey

Mark, a 19-year-old college student, had been dealing with severe cystic acne for several years. Acne had taken a toll on his self-esteem, affecting his social interactions and academic performance. Desperate for a solution, Mark's dermatologist recommended

Neo Medrol as part of a comprehensive treatment plan.

Initially, Mark was skeptical, having tried various treatments in the past with limited success. However, as he diligently followed the prescribed regimen and combined Neo Medrol with other treatments, he experienced a transformation. Over time, his cystic acne significantly improved, and the frequency of painful flare-ups decreased. Mark was grateful to Neo Medrol for providing him with a sense of control over his skin and the renewed confidence to pursue his goals fearlessly.

Sarah's Testimonial

Sarah, a 29-year-old mother, struggled with hormonal acne that often worsened during stressful periods. Her busy life left little time for extensive skincare routines, making Neo Medrol an attractive option due to its simplicity and ease of use.

With Neo Medrol, Sarah found relief from her hormonal breakouts, and the medication's antibacterial and anti-inflammatory properties helped prevent new acne from forming. As a result, she felt more confident and at ease in her role as a mother, knowing that her skin was in good hands with Neo Medrol's support.

Evan's Acne Journey

Evan, an 18-year-old student-athlete, faced the challenge of managing acne while juggling his studies and sports commitments. Acne breakouts often made him feel self-conscious, especially during games and competitions.

After incorporating Neo Medrol into his daily routine, Evan experienced a reduction in acne-related inflammation, allowing him to focus more on his athletic pursuits without the distraction of skin concerns. The convenience of Neo Medrol's topical application made it easy for Evan to maintain consistent use, and he was thrilled with the results it delivered.

These are just a few examples of how Neo Medrol has positively impacted the lives of individuals dealing with acne. Each story illustrates the power of Neo Medrol's combination of neomycin and methylprednisolone in tackling the bacterial and inflammatory aspects of acne, leading to improved skin and enhanced self-confidence.

Remember that results may vary from person to person, and individual responses to Neo Medrol can differ. If you are considering using Neo Medrol, consult a healthcare professional to determine if it is the right option for your acne management needs.

CONCLUSION - EMPOWERING CLEARER AND HEALTHIER SKIN

Throughout this book, we have explored Neo Medrol as a valuable tool in the management of acne and related skin conditions. From understanding the basics of acne and the role of Neo Medrol in treatment to delving into its composition, mode of action, and clinical studies supporting its efficacy, we have gained comprehensive insights into this topical medication.

We learned that Neo Medrol's unique combination of neomycin and methylprednisolone provides a multifaceted approach to addressing acne. By targeting both bacterial infection and inflammation, Neo Medrol offers a comprehensive solution for individuals dealing with mild to moderate forms of acne.

When using Neo Medrol, we emphasized the importance of following proper usage guidelines, including recommended dosages, application methods, and treatment duration. Alongside Neo Medrol, we explored long-term management strategies to maintain clear skin, such as adopting a consistent skincare routine, practicing sun protection, managing stress, and being mindful of diet.

Throughout the book, we were inspired by the real-life success stories and testimonials from individuals who experienced positive transformations with the help of Neo Medrol. These stories serve as a reminder of the significant impact that clearer skin can have on one's self-esteem, confidence, and overall well-being.

As we conclude this journey, it is essential to remember that skincare is not one-size-fits-all. Everyone's skin is unique, and what works for one person may not work for another. If you are considering using Neo Medrol or any other acne treatment, it is crucial to consult a healthcare professional or dermatologist. They can assess your skin condition, provide personalized recommendations, and monitor your progress throughout your acne management journey.

In embracing the knowledge gained from this book and partnering with your healthcare professional, you can empower yourself to make informed decisions about managing your acne. Whether you are starting your journey with Neo Medrol or exploring other treatment options, remember that achieving clearer and healthier skin is attainable with dedication, patience, and the right support.

May this knowledge serve as a guiding light on your path to clearer and healthier skin, enabling you to face each day with confidence and self-assurance. Remember that your skin is a reflection of your inner beauty and uniqueness, and caring for it is a powerful act of self-care and self-love.

Wishing you a successful and fulfilling acne management journey with the support of Neo Medrol and the expert guidance of your healthcare professional. Here's to a brighter, clearer, and healthier future ahead!

THE END

Printed in Great Britain
by Amazon

27015020R00030